# Planes

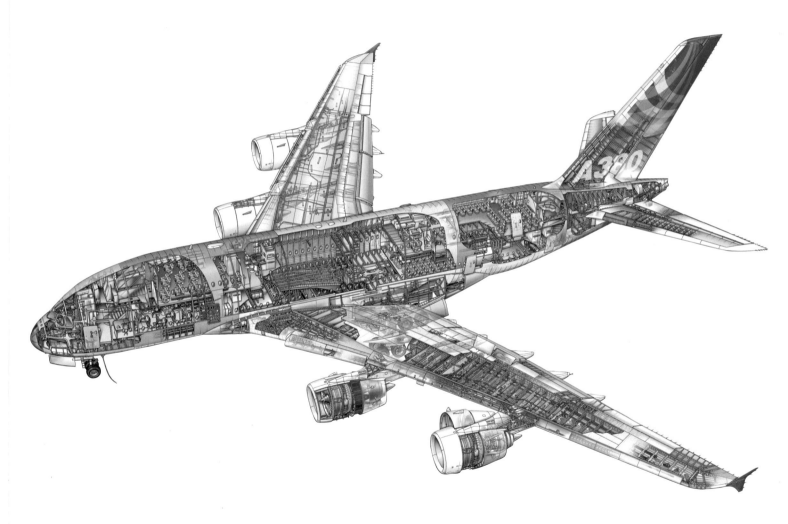

## Chris Oxlade

WAYLAND

# Planes inside out

An aeroplane is an amazingly complex machine. It is made up of thousands of parts, from tiny electronic components in the cockpit to giant pieces of metal in the wings. This plane is an Airbus A380, which is the world's largest airliner. It is 73 metres long and 80 metres across. This illustration shows all its major parts.

## Fuselage

This is the main part of the aircraft, and where the passengers sit. The tubular frame has a skin made of metal.

## Cockpit

This is where the pilots sit. It contains flying controls, computers and other electronic instruments that help the pilots to fly and navigate the aircraft.

## Landing gear

The landing gear lets the plane roll along the ground. There are five sets of wheels under the fuselage or wings and under the nose.

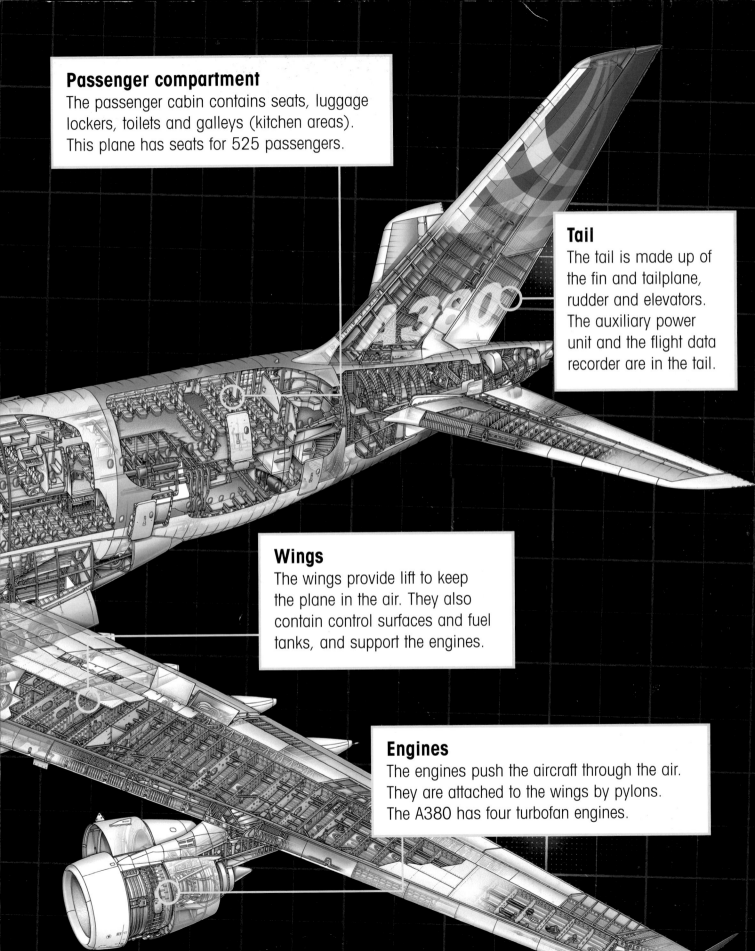

**Passenger compartment**
The passenger cabin contains seats, luggage lockers, toilets and galleys (kitchen areas). This plane has seats for 525 passengers.

**Tail**
The tail is made up of the fin and tailplane, rudder and elevators. The auxiliary power unit and the flight data recorder are in the tail.

**Wings**
The wings provide lift to keep the plane in the air. They also contain control surfaces and fuel tanks, and support the engines.

**Engines**
The engines push the aircraft through the air. They are attached to the wings by pylons. The A380 has four turbofan engines.

# Fuselage structure

This plane has a semi monocoque fuselage. This means that the fuselage of an airliner is a tube, which is a very strong shape. It is often made up of a metal skin on top of a metal frame. Modern aircraft are made from advanced materials called composites, such as glass-fibre and carbon-fibre reinforced plastic. These are stronger and lighter than metals.

Skin

## Frames, stringers and skin

The internal frame is made up of hoops called ribs around the fuselage and rods, called stringers, along the fuselage. The skin is attached to the outside of the frame. The two passenger decks and the cargo deck make the fuselage even stronger.

## Aircraft construction

In an aircraft factory, the fuselage is made in giant sections. The sections are then joined end to end to make up the finished fuselage. This is one of the sections that make up an Airbus A380 fuselage.

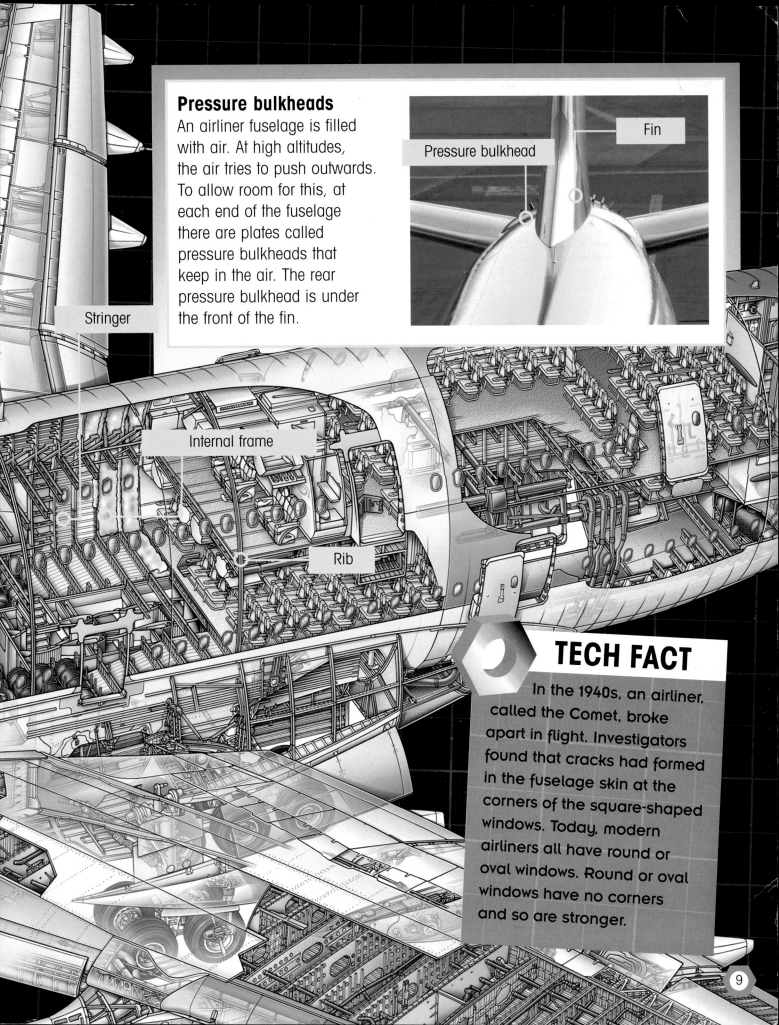

## Pressure bulkheads

An airliner fuselage is filled with air. At high altitudes, the air tries to push outwards. To allow room for this, at each end of the fuselage there are plates called pressure bulkheads that keep in the air. The rear pressure bulkhead is under the front of the fin.

Pressure bulkhead

Fin

Stringer

Internal frame

Rib

## TECH FACT

In the 1940s, an airliner, called the Comet, broke apart in flight. Investigators found that cracks had formed in the fuselage skin at the corners of the square-shaped windows. Today, modern airliners all have round or oval windows. Round or oval windows have no corners and so are stronger.

# Flying surfaces

The wings and tail of an aircraft are called its flying surfaces. As the aircraft flies through the air, the wings make an upward force, called lift. This lift supports the aircraft. The tail is made up of the vertical fin and the horizontal tailplane. It keeps the aircraft flying straight and level. The wings are extremely strong. On the ground they support the weight of the engines.

## Inside a wing

A wing is formed of a frame covered with a skin. The frame is made up of spars that run along the length of the wing, and ribs that go from front to back. There are normally two spars, a front spar and a rear spar, although some large, modern airplanes have three. The spars and ribs form the sides of boxes inside the wing, called wing boxes. Some of these boxes are used as fuel tanks.

## TECH FACT

Although wings are very strong, they can bend upwards and downwards. On the ground, the wings bend down because they are holding up the engines. In flight, they bend upwards because they are holding up the fuselage. The tip of a large wing can bend more than 7 metres.

## Tailplane structure

The structure of the fin and the tailplane is similar to that of the wings. Inside are spars and ribs, and outside is a skin of metal. The rudder and ailerons are made of lightweight materials and are moved by hydraulic rams called actuators.

Fin

Tailplane

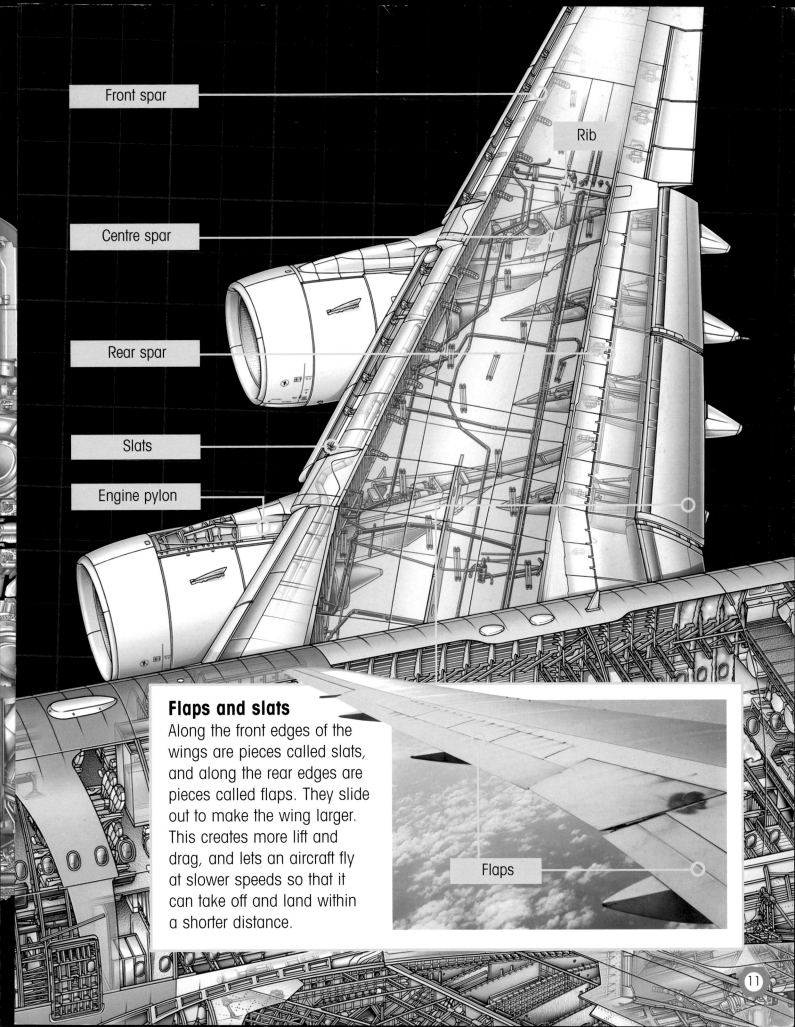

Front spar

Rib

Centre spar

Rear spar

Slats

Engine pylon

### Flaps and slats
Along the front edges of the
wings are pieces called slats,
and along the rear edges are
pieces called flaps. They slide
out to make the wing larger.
This creates more lift and
drag, and lets an aircraft fly
at slower speeds so that it
can take off and land within
a shorter distance.

Flaps

# Servicing and fuelling

A jet engine needs many extra parts to keep it working. For example, it needs pipes and pumps to take fuel to the combustion chamber, and oil to keep the parts moving smoothly. Most turbofan engines also have thrust reversers, which are used on landing. They fold out and deflect the jet exhaust forwards, slowing the aircraft down.

### Engine servicing

Just like a car engine, an aircraft engine must be carefully looked after so that it keeps working properly and does not break down. Inspection covers open up to let engineers look at the insides of the engine. If an engine breaks down and cannot be fixed, it is changed for a new one.

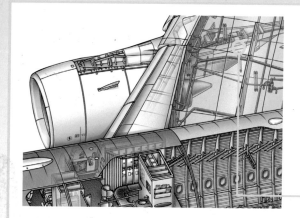

### Engine fuel

Turbofan engines and other jet engines use a special type of fuel called aviation fuel. The most common aviation fuel is called JET A-1. On an airliner, the fuel is stored in tanks inside the wings. It is pumped into the wings from a fuel tanker or underground storage tanks.

Fuel tank

Auxiliary power unit

## Auxiliary power unit exhaust

Large aircraft have an extra engine called an auxiliary power unit (APU). This small jet engine provides power to start the main engines and electricity for the aircraft when the main engines are not running. The A380 has its APU exhaust in the tail.

# Military jet engines

Combat aircraft are also powered by jet engines. Most of them have turbofans, like airliners, but a few have turbojets instead. These jet engines do not have a large fan like a turbofan. One or two engines are placed inside or underneath the fuselage. This lets the aircraft roll quickly from side to side so it can make quick turns to attack enemy planes or make an escape.

## Thrust and weight

Combat aircraft such as this F-18 need to accelerate and climb quickly, so they have very powerful engines. Most modern fighters have engines that produce more thrust than their own weight. With engines on full power, they can climb straight up.

## Afterburners

The glow at the back of this fighter comes from its afterburner. Here, fuel is injected into the hot exhaust gases from the engine. The fuel burns, producing more hot gases and extra thrust. Pilots use their afterburners in short bursts for quick take-offs and fast climbs.

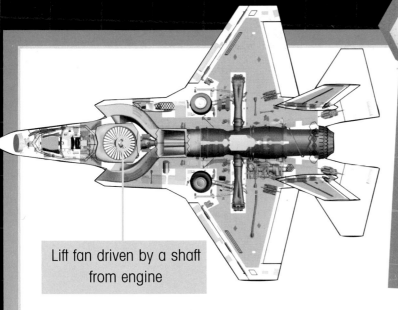

It would be impossible for the pilot to fly the F-35B without the help of on-board computers. In vertical flight, the computers control the thrust from each of the nozzles and the lift fan. Very accurate control is essential to keep the aircraft from flipping over.

Lift fan driven by a shaft from engine

## Vertical flight

The Lockheed Martin F-35B is a short take-off and vertical landing (STOVL) combat aircraft. The engine produces forward thrust for normal flight and downward thrust for take-off and vertical landings. For vertical landings, the rear nozzle bends to point downwards. The engine exhaust comes from the rear nozzle and from two small nozzles under the wings. More vertical thrust comes from the lift fan behind the cockpit.

Doors open to allow air into the lift fan

# Landing gear

All aircraft need landing gear (also called undercarriage) for take-off and landing. The main landing gear of most modern aircraft is under the wings or fuselage, and a nose wheel under the nose. This is known as a tricycle undercarriage. During flight, the landing gear retracts (folds away) into landing gear compartments, which are covered with folding doors.

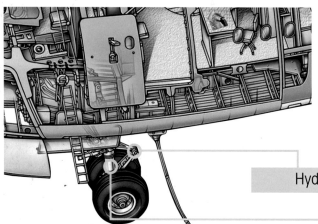

## Struts and locks

The landing gear wheels are on the end of sturdy legs. The legs are raised and lowered by hydraulic rams. Struts lock the legs in place to stop them wobbling. There are shock absorbers inside the legs to soak up bumps when the aircraft lands.

Hydraulic rams

Shock absorbers

## Ready to land

A pilot lowers the landing gear a few minutes before an aircraft lands. The legs fold down and lock into place. Indicator lights in the cockpit will then show that the landing gear is properly down. This Boeing 747 has four sets of main wheels. On the ground, the nose wheel is used to steer the aircraft.

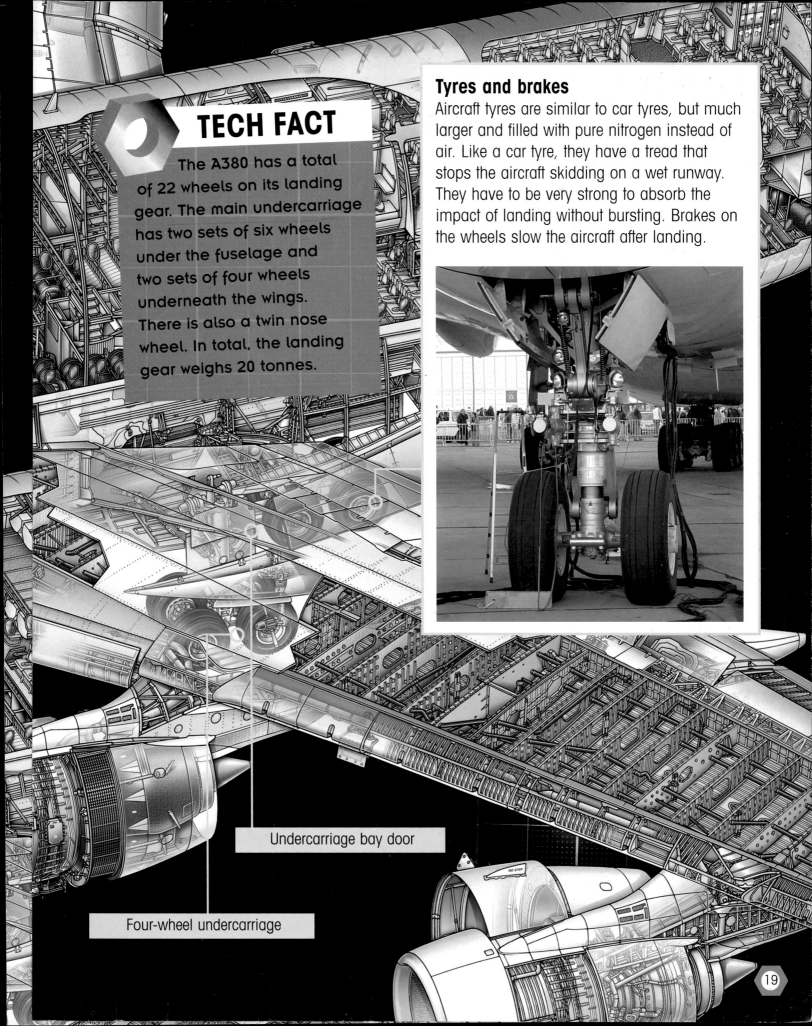

## TECH FACT

The A380 has a total of 22 wheels on its landing gear. The main undercarriage has two sets of six wheels under the fuselage and two sets of four wheels underneath the wings. There is also a twin nose wheel. In total, the landing gear weighs 20 tonnes.

## Tyres and brakes

Aircraft tyres are similar to car tyres, but much larger and filled with pure nitrogen instead of air. Like a car tyre, they have a tread that stops the aircraft skidding on a wet runway. They have to be very strong to absorb the impact of landing without bursting. Brakes on the wheels slow the aircraft after landing.

Undercarriage bay door

Four-wheel undercarriage

The flight deck is the area at the front of the fuselage where the pilots sit. There are normally two seats side by side on the flight deck. They are surrounded by controls for flying and for operating the aircraft's systems. There are also lights, dials and screens that show information about the aircraft.

## Flying controls

The pilots' main flying controls are the control column and rudder pedals. They move hinged control surfaces, the ailerons on the wings, the elevators on the tailplane and the rudder on the fin. These surfaces make the aircraft turn, climb or descend. In the nose of the aircraft are computers and other electronics, called avionics, which help the pilots to fly and navigate, such as the autopilot.

## TECH FACT

Most modern airliners, including the Airbus A380, have a flight control system called fly by wire. This means that a computer is in control of the ailerons, elevators, rudder and engines. The pilot decides when to turn, climb or descend, but the computer actually flies the aircraft.

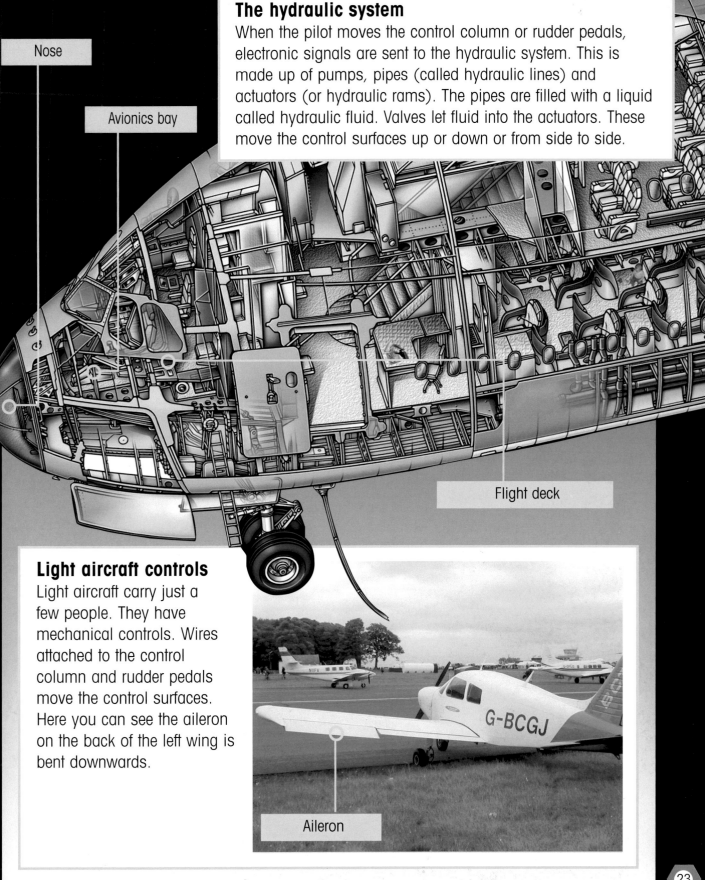

## The hydraulic system

When the pilot moves the control column or rudder pedals, electronic signals are sent to the hydraulic system. This is made up of pumps, pipes (called hydraulic lines) and actuators (or hydraulic rams). The pipes are filled with a liquid called hydraulic fluid. Valves let fluid into the actuators. These move the control surfaces up or down or from side to side.

Nose

Avionics bay

Flight deck

## Light aircraft controls

Light aircraft carry just a few people. They have mechanical controls. Wires attached to the control column and rudder pedals move the control surfaces. Here you can see the aileron on the back of the left wing is bent downwards.

G-BCGJ

Aileron

# Emergency!

Aircraft such as the A380 are very safe. Even so, they have many parts that help the crew and passengers in case of an emergency. These include oxygen masks, emergency lights and escape slides. There are also systems that stop pilots making mistakes. For example, the ground proximity warning sounds an alarm if the aircraft flies too low.

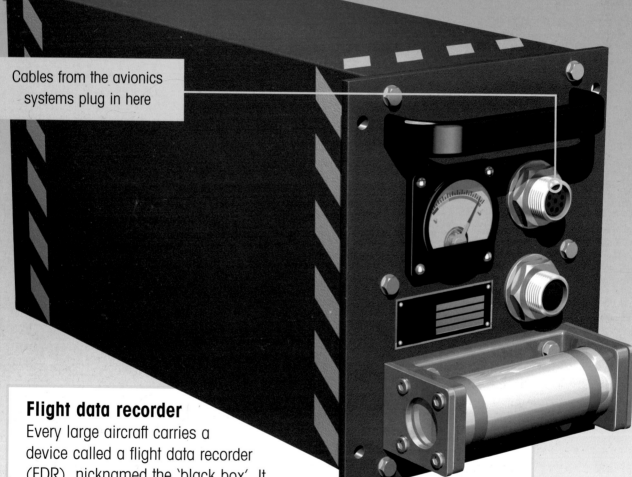

Cables from the avionics systems plug in here

### Flight data recorder
Every large aircraft carries a device called a flight data recorder (FDR), nicknamed the 'black box'. It records details about a flight, such as altitude and speed, and what the pilots are saying to each other. The FDR is in a strong metal container in the aircraft's tail. If an aircraft crash lands, the information from the FDR helps investigators to find out what happened in the moments before the accident.

## Ejection seats

In a combat aircraft, the pilot sits in an ejection seat. If the aircraft is going to crash, the pilot pulls a handle and the seat blasts out of the cockpit. First, the cockpit's glass canopy is released and flies into the air. Then small rockets fire the seat upwards. When the seat is clear of the aircraft, a parachute comes out and the seat floats to the ground. It takes less than a second for the pilot to be ejected.

## Cabin equipment

There is an oxygen mask above each seat in the cabin. If the cabin air pressure falls at high altitude, the masks drop down, giving passengers oxygen so that they can breathe. There are lifejackets under each seat in case the aircraft has to land in water. The cabin doors contain inflatable escape slides and life rafts.

# Helicopter parts

On the inside of a helicopter are some parts that are similar to an airliner, and some parts that are very different. The structure of the fuselage is like an airliner, with a metal frame covered with a skin. Inside are seats, a cockpit and avionics. The main difference is that the engines are on top of the fuselage. They drive a rotor that lifts the helicopter into the air.

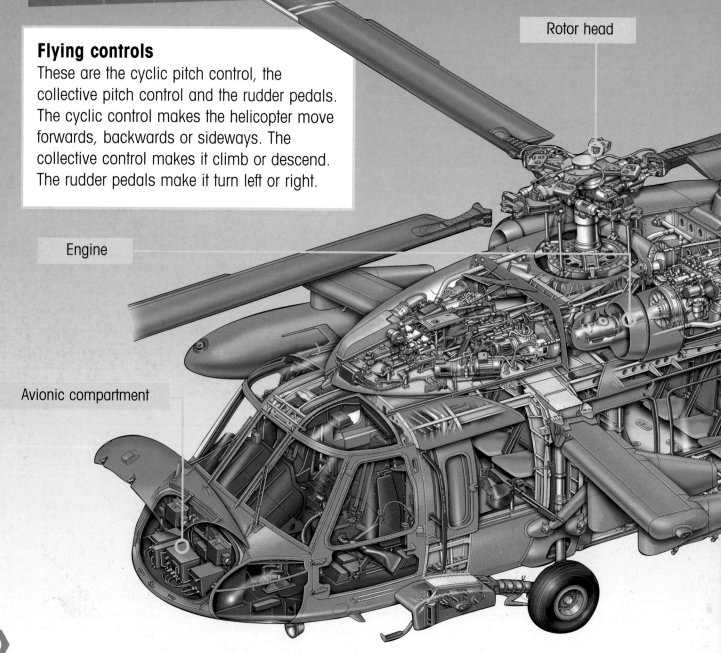

Rotor head

### Flying controls
These are the cyclic pitch control, the collective pitch control and the rudder pedals. The cyclic control makes the helicopter move forwards, backwards or sideways. The collective control makes it climb or descend. The rudder pedals make it turn left or right.

Engine

Avionic compartment